The European Discovery of New Zealand: The History and Legacy of Early Expeditions and British Settlements on New Zealand

By Charles River Editors

A mid-19th century painting of a Scottish Highland family in New Zealand

About Charles River Editors

Charles River Editors is a boutique digital publishing company, specializing in bringing history back to life with educational and engaging books on a wide range of topics. Keep up to date with our new and free offerings with [this 5 second sign up on our weekly mailing list](), and visit [Our Kindle Author Page]() to see other recently published Kindle titles.

We make these books for you and always want to know our readers' opinions, so we encourage you to leave reviews and look forward to publishing new and exciting titles each week.

Introduction

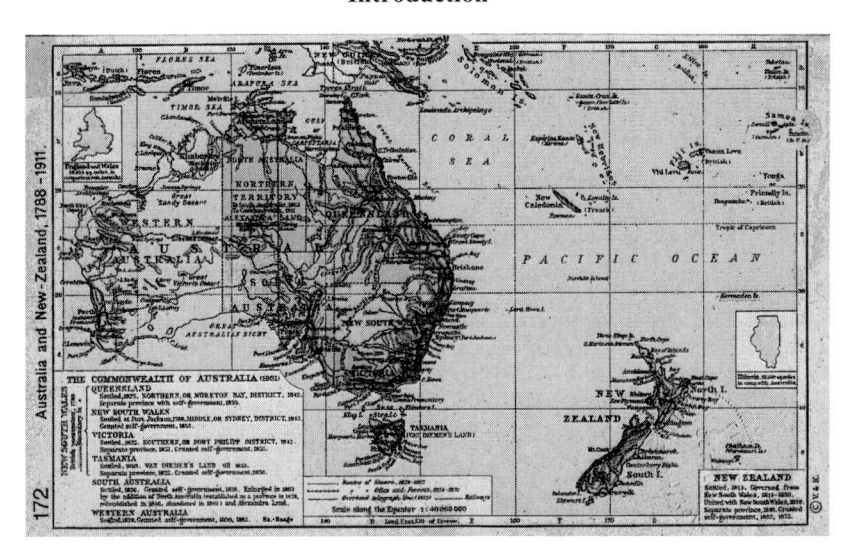

The Settlement of New Zealand

"When one house dies, a second lives." - Māori proverb

By the mid-17th century, the existence of a land in the south referred to as Terra Australis was generally known and understood by the Europeans, and incrementally, its shores were observed and mapped. Van Diemen's Land, an island off the south coast of Australia now called Tasmania, was identified in 1642 by Dutch mariner Abel Tasman, and a few months later, the intrepid Dutchman would add New Zealand to the map of the known world.

At the time, the English were the greatest naval power in Europe, but they arrived on the scene rather later. The first to appear was William Dampier, captain of the HMS Roebuck, in 1699, after he had been granted a Royal Commission by King William III to explore the east coast of New Holland. By then, the general global balance of power was shifting, and with the English gaining a solid foothold in India, their supremacy in the Indian Ocean trade zone began. The Dutch, once predominant in the region, began slowly to lose ground, slipping out of contention as a major global trading power. So too were the Portuguese, also once dominant in the region. It was now just the French and the English who were facing one another down in a quest to dominate the world, but their imperial interests were focused mainly in India and the East Indies, as well as the Caribbean and the Americas. As a result, the potential of a vast, practically uninhabited great southern continent did not yet hold much interest.

By then the world was largely mapped, with just regions such as the Arctic Archipelago and the two poles remaining terra incognita. A few gaps needed to be filled in here and there, but all of the essential details were known. At the same time, a great deal of imperial energy was at play in Europe, particularly in Britain. Britain stood at the cusp of global dominance thanks almost entirely to the Royal Navy, which emerged in the 17th and 18th centuries as an institution significantly more than the sum of its parts. With vast assets available even in peacetime, expeditions of science and explorations were launched in every direction. This was done not only to claim ownership of the field of global exploration, but also to undercut the imperial ambitions of others, in particular the French.

In 1769, Captain James Cook's historic expedition in the region would lead to an English claim on Australia, but before he reached Australia, he sailed near New Zealand and spent weeks mapping part of New Zealand's coast. Cook later asserted that the only major sources of timber and flax in the Pacific region were to be found in New Zealand and Norfolk Island, which would prove crucial to the British Empire and the Royal Navy in particular, and Cook also provided a firsthand account of a tense standoff with New Zealand's indigenous natives on the shoreline. Over the next 90 years, Cook's journey and his account would lay the basis for British activities in the region, and those activities would forge the modern history of New Zealand at a great cost.

The European Discovery of New Zealand: The History and Legacy of Early Expeditions and British Settlements on New Zealand analyzes the expeditions that discovered New Zealand and the early settlements and conflicts waged there from 1650-1850. Along with pictures of important people, places, and events, you will learn about the European settlement of New Zealand like never before.

The European Discovery of New Zealand: The History and Legacy of Early Expeditions and British Settlements on New Zealand

About Charles River Editors

Introduction

   New Zealand's First Arrivals

   The Musket Wars

   Missionaries and Whalers

   The Founding of a Colony

   Immigration and Settlement

   The New Zealand Wars

   Colonial Government

   Appendix: The Treaty of Waitangi

   Online Resources

   Bibliography

Free Books by Charles River Editors

Discounted Books by Charles River Editors

New Zealand's First Arrivals

On December 13, 1642, a Dutch survey expedition led by Abel Tasman and comprised of two ships, *Heemskerck* and *Zeehaen*, encountered in the South Pacific what Tasman later described as "a large land uplifted high." What Tasman was in fact looking at was the South Island of New Zealand, and the uplifted high land consisted of the Southern Alps. This land Tasman declared "*Staten Landt*," or "State Land," and a few days later the small flotilla drifted into Cook Strait.[1] There the two ships anchored in a natural harbor now known as "*Mohua*," or as it is known today, Golden Bay. There Tasman found a deeply indented shoreline and calm waters, fringed by wooded hills, and gifted with a mild and temperate climate. It certainly was a pleasing sight, and Tasman earmarked it as a country perfectly suited to future European settlement.

A contemporary portrait believed to depict Tasman and his family

Then, quite unexpectedly, this utopian aspect was shattered when a flotilla of war canoes detached itself from shore and rushed out to meet them. A brief skirmish followed, and a few Dutch sailors were killed before a round of shots was fired that immediately dispersed the

---
[1] There are different versions of this naming. Another is that Tasman believed it to be connected to Argentina's Staten Island, or *Isla de los Estados*.

attackers. The sides separated and the natives returned to shore. They had never encountered ballistics before, so the experience undoubtedly scared them, but Tasman quickly hoisted sail and hurried back to open water. He later wrote of the encounter, "In the evening about one hour after sunset we saw many lights on land and four vessels near the shore, two of which betook themselves towards us. When our two boats returned to the ships reporting that they had found not less than thirteen fathoms of water, and with the sinking of the sun (which sank behind the high land) they had been still about half a mile from the shore. After our people had been on board about one glass, people in the two canoes began to call out to us in gruff, hollow voices. We could not in the least understand any of it; however, when they called out again several times we called back to them as a token answer. But they did not come nearer than a stone's shot. They also blew many times on an instrument, which produced a sound like the moors' trumpets. We had one of our sailors (who could play somewhat on the trumpet) play some tunes to them in answer."

Tasman named the place Murderer's Bay and continued on, arriving next in the Tongan Archipelago. To the Dutch captain, who had already touched the shores of *Terra Australis*, or "New Holland" as he left it, this first encounter with the natives of New Zealand was sobering. The Australian Aboriginals he had previously met were either friendly or semi-wild, fleeing to the bush like hares at the first sight of a white man. He had certainly never expected to be met on shore by a war party, and he immediately understood that anyone attempting to conquer and settle this land would certainly need to be prepared to fight for it.

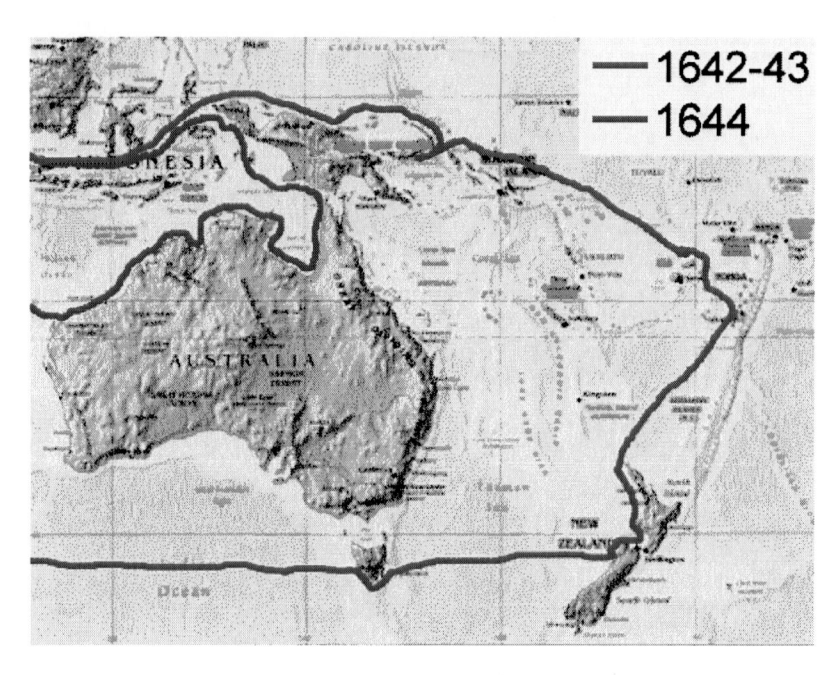

A map of Tasman's voyages in the region

A contemporary depiction of Murderer's Bay

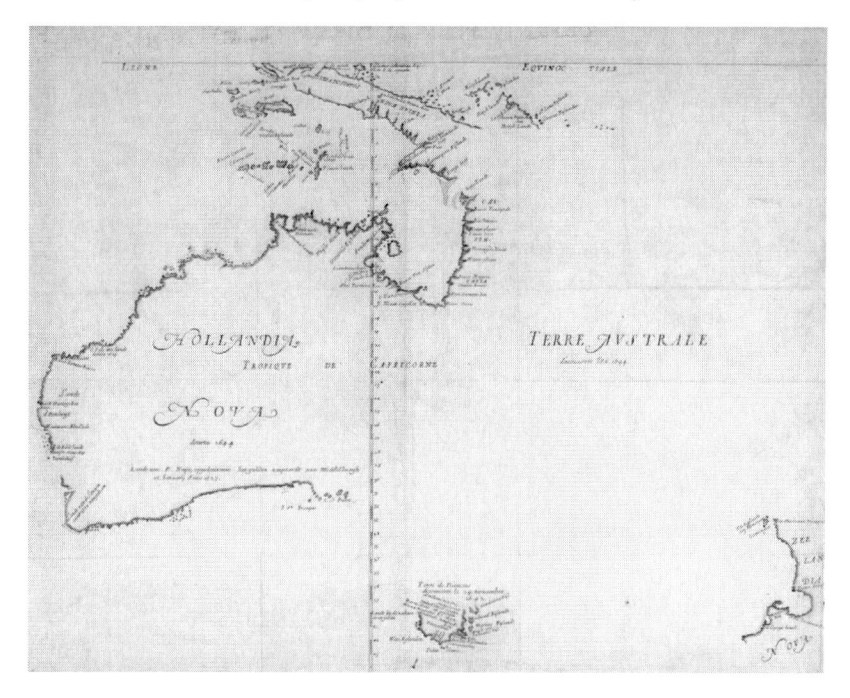

A 1645 map of the region

Archeologists have since explained this initial encounter as the unexpected arrival of an entirely unknown race into an area of settlement and agriculture, and the natural impulse that the indigenous people would feel to protect it. Nonetheless, this first European encounter with the Māori must certainly have presented a striking and intimidating picture. Warlike and tribal, the Māori were then, as they are now, flamboyant and decorative, fond of rituals and ceremonies, and accustomed to warfare as a cultural expression and means of inhabiting an accommodating land. Their distinctive tattoos, both erotic and totemic, were unique and striking expressions of a robust and violent, but also deeply accomplished society.

A 19th century depiction of Māoris

Historians can still only estimate when the first people reached Australia, but Māoris are known to have begun making landfall in New Zealand less than 1,000 years ago, around the early 14th century. According to local lore, "Kupe," the first Polynesian mariner to arrive on New Zealand's shores, is typically described today as an "explorer," which implies a systematic search for new lands. Kupe's home, however, was the island of "Hawaiki," a mythical island from where the Polynesian race originated, and these origins tend to flavor Kupe's odyssey with the elements of a genesis story. Nonetheless, it was at about that time the Polynesians began to settle on New Zealand. Riding the currents of the South Pacific Gyre, and following the stars, the first arrivals came across more than 2,600 miles of ocean in large ocean-going canoes known as *waka*. The origins of this migration are somewhere in the region of French Polynesia, Tahiti, and the Cook and Society Islands. Currents and wind patterns deposited them eventually on North Island, from which there was little hope of return. Others soon followed, and as the generations progressed, a settled community took root.

There are a number of theories in regards to the style and pattern of this migration, but in essence the two main hypotheses suggest either a piecemeal movement or a single, "Great Fleet." Generally, it is the latter that is the more popular theory. This, of course, implies, at the very least, the confidence and skill of an accomplished maritime people, strong leadership, and a firm objective.

The Polynesians can trace their origins to south Asia, migrating over thousands of years from the coast and islands of China, along the Malay Archipelago, and across the South Pacific in an arc that would inevitably deposit them on the islands of New Zealand.[2] According to the "Great Fleet" theory, an expedition of at least seven canoes, carrying several hundred crew and passengers, was inspired by the reports of Kupe, and later the Polynesian explorers Toi and Whātonga, with the first substantial landfall taking place within a few years of 1280. A more ancient, nomadic people called *Moriori* were already present on North Island, but they were quickly wiped out by this invasion of aggressive and warlike Polynesians, who called themselves "Māori," or the "First People."[3]

This is the orthodox version of how the Māori came to be present in New Zealand, and if Abel Tasman had been granted the opportunity to look more closely at Māori society, what he would have found would have been an advanced, organized and adaptable people, warlike in disposition but agricultural. This was fortunate, because the incoming Māori found themselves stranded on a landscape and climate very different from that which they were accustomed. It required sturdier homes, more comprehensive clothing, and styles of agriculture more appropriate to a temperate climate. This process of adaption took time, but it was made quite a lot easier by the sheer bounty of the land, which had shorelines teeming with fish and interior landscapes populated by game. The first settlements congregated in the estuaries and around the river mouths of North Island, and the great flightless bird, the Moa, was an easy prey to hunt and could be found all over the place. Although hunted to extinction before the year 1500, the Moa nonetheless offered the Māori a vital bridge to the development of local agriculture.

As the centuries passed, the Māori gradually dispersed across both islands, slowly evolving their unique lifestyle and culture. As many Europeans would observe, however, a significant part of that culture revolved around warfare. Clans and tribes (*iwi*) began to separate, and soon enough they were at odds with one another. Before long, a revolving tradition of war took root, and from this tradition a "god of war" emerged, variously named *Tūmatauenga, Kahukura, Uenuku*, and *Maru*. The causes of war were often based on land and natural resources, but also based on revenge, slaves and sometimes tradition. A word – *"mana"* – evolved, which, in idiomatic terms, means something akin to spirituality, the "kismet" of victory and power. This ideology elevated warfare to something higher than the usual temporal pursuits of land, slaves and grievances, and towards something almost on the level of a religion.

On a practical, day-to-day level, Māori culture, although Stone Age, was nonetheless highly developed, especially in comparison to the Aboriginal communities of neighboring Australia. The Māori were of Polynesian origin, and their cultural peculiarities have tended to reflect that.

---

[2] The current theory, based on mitochondrial DNA, is that the Māori can trace their ancient origins to Taiwanese aboriginals some 5,200 years ago.

[3] Fresh archaeological evidence now suggests that the Moriori were a subgroup of mainland Māori, who migrated from New Zealand to the Chatham Islands, there developing their own distinctive, peaceful culture. This again is a contested theory.

Many of their implements were made of stone, at least partly, but the preferred materials were wood, ivory and bone. Everything from bird to whale bones, and indeed human bones, were used in constructing items as diverse as hoes, needles, and war clubs. Many types of hardwood were to be found on the island, and weapons of war were often wooden. It was a society rich in totems, and the varied depiction of these laid the foundation of a strong artistic tradition, featuring wood carving, body decoration, theater and oratory, and multiple rituals and ceremonies. Māori architecture was artistic, and reasonably advanced, while society was generally patrilineal, and the strongest political unit was the iwi.

A 19th century portrait of a Māori

Within a century or two of their arrival, the rival clans and iwi began to consolidate, confederate, and establish recognized and understood boundaries. The cult of warfare, thereafter, settled into a pattern not dissimilar to the great European estates of the Middle Ages. There was constant jostling for influence and authority, and a great deal of posturing and ceremony began to surround the business of war, which in due course became largely ceremonial itself.

A multilateral balance of power thus settled on the land, and a balanced social order was maintained, based on land and natural resources.

All of this, however, was shattered when the first substantive contact with European explorers took place.

The Musket Wars

"I have always found them of a brave, noble, open and benevolent disposition, but they are a people that will never put up with an insult if they have an opportunity to resent it." – Captain James Cook

The first map to feature the name *Nova Zeelandia* was published by the Dutch in 1645, but no substantive European effort was made to exploit or visit this territory until at least a century later. After Abel Tasman, the next recorded European visit would be that of Captain James Cook.

In 1767, the Royal Society persuaded King George III to allocate funds for it to send an astronomer to the Pacific, and on January 1, 1768, the London Annual Register reported, "Mr. Banks, Dr. Solander, and Mr. Green the astronomer, set out for Deal, to embark on board the Endeavour, Captain Cook, for the South Seas, under the direction of the royal society, to observe the transit of Venus next summer, and to make discoveries." Mr. Banks was Joseph Banks, a botanist, and he brought along Dr. Daniel Solander, a Swedish naturalist. Charles Green was at that time the assistant to Nevil Maskelyne, the Astronomer Royal. The expedition, which would leave later in 1768, would be captained by Cook, a war veteran who had recently fought in the French & Indian War against the French in North America.

King George III

Banks

Solander

What the article did not mention was that the Admiralty was also hoping to find the famed Terra Australis Incognita, the legendary "unknown southern land." This came out later, when the *London Gazetteer* reported on August 18, 1768, "The gentlemen, who are to sail in a few days for George's Land, the new discovered island in the Pacific ocean, with an intention to observe the Transit of Venus, are likewise, we are credibly informed, to attempt some new discoveries in that vast unknown tract, above the latitude 40."

When Cook's expedition began in 1768, it included more than 80 men, consisting of 73 sailors and 12 members of the Royal Marines. Presumably, the expedition was supposed to be for entirely scientific – and hence peaceful – purposes. The *Endeavour* left Plymouth on August 26, 1768, and Cook landed at Matavai Bay, Tahiti, on April 13, 1769. The most important task at hand, other than day-to-day survival, was preparing to observe the transit of Venus that would occur on June 3.

Having completed the scientific assignments, the *Endeavour* next set sail in search of Terra Australis. After sailing for nearly two months, the crew earned the prize of being only the second group of Europeans to ever visit New Zealand. They arrived on October 6, 1769, and Cook described a harrowing experience when the men came ashore: "MONDAY, 9th October. …I went ashore with a Party of men in the Pinnace and yawl accompanied by Mr. Banks and Dr. Solander. We landed abreast of the Ship and on the East side of the River just mentioned; but seeing some of the Natives on the other side of the River of whom I was desirous of speaking with, and finding that we could not ford the River, I order'd the yawl in to carry us over, and the pinnace to lay at the Entrance. In the mean time the Indians made off. However we went as far as their Hutts which lay about 2 or 300 Yards from the water side, leaving 4 boys to take care of the Yawl, which we had no sooner left than 4 Men came out of the woods on the other side the River, and would certainly have cut her off had not the People in the Pinnace discover'd them and called to her to drop down the Stream, which they did, being closely persued by the Indians. The coxswain of the Pinnace, who had the charge of the Boats, seeing this, fir'd 2 Musquets over their Heads; the first made them stop and Look round them, but the 2nd they took no notice of; upon which a third was fir'd and kill'd one of them upon the Spot just as he was going to dart his spear at the Boat. At this the other 3 stood motionless for a Minute or two, seemingly quite surprised; wondering, no doubt, what it was that had thus kill'd their Comrade; but as soon as they recovered themselves they made off, dragging the Dead body a little way and then left it. Upon our hearing the report of the Musquets we immediately repair'd to the Boats, and after viewing the Dead body we return'd on board."

Over the following weeks, Cook devoted himself to making a detailed map of the New Zealand coast. Sailing west, Cook hoped to reach Van Diemen's Land, known today as Tasmania, but instead, the winds forced him north, leading him and his men to the southeastern coast of Australia.

Cook

A replica of Cook's ship, *Endeavour*

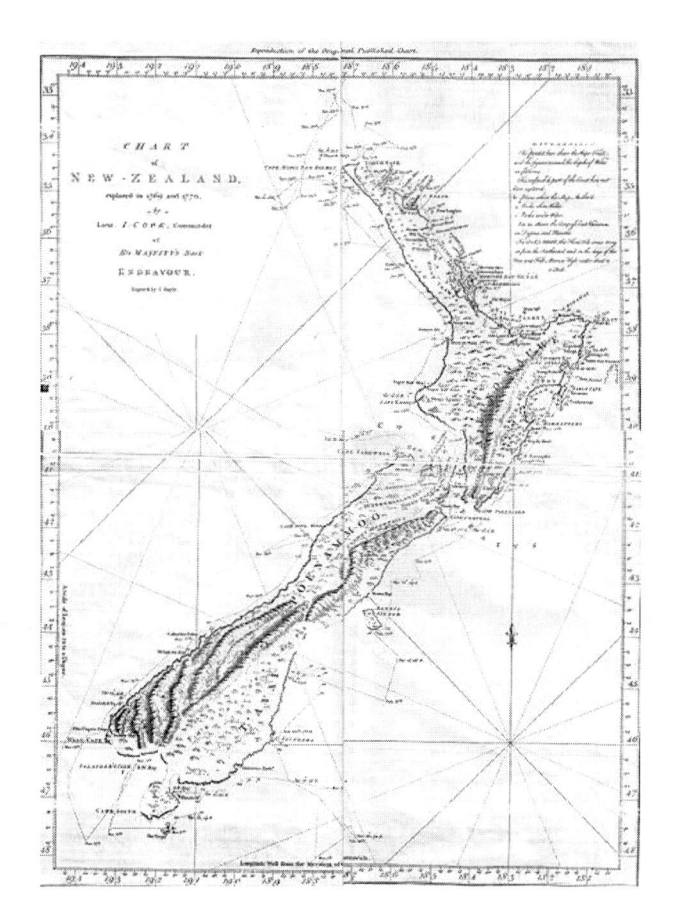

Cook's map of New Zealand's shore

    Thus, it was Cook who would Anglicize the name to New Zealand, and on both of his subsequent voyages, Cook returned to New Zealand, but only to cruise the coast and touch lightly on the shore.

    Cook's expedition may have been for the purposes of science on the surface, but when he claimed the new territory, the British realized it might serve as a center of future British maritime power and trade in the region. Indeed, as it turned out, that region that would soon be of significant interest to the British because of the American Revolution.

    The American colonists, although patriotic and committed, could never have taken on the

British Empire unassisted. A vast anti-British coalition formed in Europe, which provided the political, economic and material bulwark of the Revolution. Russia's Catherine the Great was the prime mover in what came to be known as the League of Armed Neutrality, which facilitated the free flow of money and materiel to North America, provided as aid and assistance by the non-belligerent powers. These, although hardly non-belligerent, included France, which was almost never unwilling to oppose the English, as well as Prussia, the Holy Roman Empire, the Netherlands, Portugal, Spain, and Ottoman Turkey.

After the 1783 Treaty of Paris, the British and the new United States somewhat reconciled, while the French, Dutch, and Spanish continued their bitterly anti-English campaign. In combination, they outstripped British maritime power, and they were in a position to challenge British trade with India and China, the cornerstone of the colossal wealth machine that was British East Indian trade.

At the time, the broad pattern of British trade saw British ships embarking south from England, sailing with the currents across the Atlantic, before striking east via the Cape of Good Hope to India. They would then load up on opium grown under duress by the Indians and ship it to China, where it was sold under duress to the Chinese. For the return journey, tea and various other exotic produce from India were acquired.

Vital to this trade equation was the Cape of Good Hope, a Dutch possession since 1652, and a pivotal strategic maritime position. As far as the British were concerned, the Cape of Good Hope was, at least for the time being, the weak link in the chain. The Dutch were allied with the French, and in addition to the Cape of Good Hope, the Dutch also held the important Ceylonese port of Trincomalee, from which they and their French allies were in a position to threaten British India and British trade interests throughout the region.

If push came to shove and the Cape of Good Hope became unavailable, the British trading fleet would be forced to utilize the east coast of South America, dealing with numerous Spanish and Spanish allied regimes inimical to the British, after which the Cape Horn or Magellan Straits would require negotiation before the long haul across the South Pacific to India. This would certainly not have been ideal.

Then there was the more subtle question of basic raw materials. The Royal Navy, the largest single maritime force in existence, had stripped the British Isles of timber reserves to the extent that a fleet of wooden ships could not be domestically sustained. British timber supplies that supported the local ship-building industries not only came mainly from Russia, but also other Baltic nations. However, in the aftermath of the American Revolution, Russia had become rather estranged and could no longer entirely be trusted. An average Royal Navy or merchant ship of the line utilized more than one mast, which was often several hundred feet tall, and these frequently required repair and replacement. So did the sails and the ships themselves. Denmark and Sweden, alternative sources of timber for the British, were also now of uncertain status, having signed on with the Russian sponsored pro-American League of Armed Neutrality.

It certainly was a hostile world for the British in the late 18th century, even as the British stood to benefit most from international trade. The Royal Navy and the British maritime fleet dominated the major maritime trade routes, but they did so from a position with almost no friends, and ultimately, if Britain could not rely on the cooperation of any other European powers, then the alternative was simply to make do alone. Cook happened to be of the opinion that the only major sources of timber and flax in the Pacific region were to be found in New Zealand and Norfolk Island, located some 1,000 miles northeast of Botany Bay. Nonetheless, it was his opinion that Botany Bay represented the most viable location for a permanent British colony.

Meanwhile, the anti-British alliance continued to ferment in the aftermath of the French Revolution. The French were deeply embittered by their ejection from North America, and for that matter, so were the British, but there was little to be gained by either side crying over spilled milk. However, the French remained deeply interested in India, which was still not comprehensively dominated by the British, and thus still vulnerable to a robust French effort at a takeover. In fact, the French were negotiating a treaty with Ottoman Egypt that would allow French use of Egyptian soil in general communication with her surviving outposts in India. Those outposts were fortified with apparently decommissioned gunships, and a military alliance was formalized with the Dutch for the use of port facilities at the Cape of Good Hope and other Dutch bases in the Pacific.

As a result, in the wake of Cook's voyages, a robust body of commercial explorers, the European whaling fleet, began to probe the New Zealand shoreline for whales and fur seals. It was they who founded the first settlements, and they made substantive contact with the Māoris. Contact in this case was more sustained and engaged, so trade took place, and goods and commodities changed hands. For the first time, the Māoris were introduced to metal, and the potential and value of trade was realized.

More importantly, the value of guns was realized, and for a martial people, this certainly must have been a seminal moment. The potential of this technology was immediately apprehended, and almost instantly the tempo and intensity of internal warfare increased. This is an era of the history of New Zealand known as the "Musket Wars," and alternatively, the "Māori Holocaust," which is probably more accurate.

The Māori began acquiring muskets in trade with itinerate whalers and seal hunters almost at the moment that the two cultures met. Later, at the turn of the 19th century, flax and timber traders from Port Jackson and Sydney began shipping in large quantities. The first internal conflicts that came about as a consequence of this were recorded in and around the northern tip of North Island, beginning in about 1807 or 1808. This was the "Battle of Moremonui," fought between the *Ngāpuhi* and *Ngāti Whātua* in Northland, not far from present-day Dargaville.

What is interesting about this brief conflict is that one side, the Ngāpuhi, had muskets, but they had not mastered their use sufficiently to overwhelm an opposing force of similar size armed with traditional weapons, and they were ultimately defeated. The early firearms that found their way into Māori hands were of very dubious quality, and generally in poor condition. Historians have tended, therefore, to describe the part played by early musketry in Māori warfare as "shock and awe." In much the same way Abel Tasman's release of a canister of shot sent the Māori scampering, so the same was true for any group encountering guns for the first time.

Before long, members of the *Ngāti Korokoro hapū* clan of Ngāpuhi were delivered a second major defeat when a raid on the neighboring *Kai Tutae* iwi was defeated despite the fact they outnumbered the enemy 10-1. This was simply because the *Kai Tutae* had equipped themselves with more and better muskets. This became the pattern, and a kind of arms race soon began. The various iwi began amassing weapons and launched heavier and more aggressive raids on one another, developing a slave economy that produced both food and flax for export, in exchange, of course, for more guns.

A secondary trade in smoked heads, or *mokomokai*, also developed as something of a byproduct of war. These satisfied the macabre curiosity of visiting Europeans, who accepted them as trade items. Before long, no governor's lodge, civil servant's office, or club bar was complete without one.[4] In part because of their value, raids were being carried out purely to acquire more heads, which were hastily preserved and sold. Prisoners of war and slaves were killed, with their heads randomly tattooed and preserved for sale. In 1931, the Governor of New South Wales, General Sir Ralph Darling, was driven by the slaughter to issue a ban on any further trade in smoked heads from New Zealand.

In 1821, Hongi Hika, *rangatira* (chief) and war leader of the Ngāpuhi, traveled to England

---

[4] *Mokomokai*, or smoked heads, was a traditional Māori practice of preserving the heads of fallen enemies, and other deceased. This was originally ceremonial, but with the rush to acquire guns, they were freely traded.

with the Anglican missionary Thomas Kendall, and on his return, called in at Sydney and traded the many gifts he had received for between 300 and 500 muskets. He then used the guns to mount raids across a much greater area.

The effects of all of this on the wider Māori society were obviously devastating. Sometime in 1835, warriors of the *Ngāti Mutunga, Ngāti Tama* and *Ngāti Toa* hijacked a British ship to carry them to the Chatham Islands, and there they fell upon and slaughtered about 10% of the Moriori, enslaving the survivors, but then descending inevitably into war between themselves.

Tactically, muskets in the hands of a detachment of marauding Māori warriors had limited offensive value, usually because they were inaccurate and the musketeers themselves had no training. Their main use, therefore, was in creating a situation of confusion to allow more traditional infantrymen to rush the enemy and defeat them with traditional weapons.

However, as proficiency and technology improved, muskets began to be employed directly in battle. Double-barrels were preferred, and occasional modifications were made. Often in battle, women were used to rapidly reload the weapons.

Until 1841, New Zealand, as a British dependency, was administered as part of New South Wales, and for the most part, wars and conflicts between different groups of Māori in New Zealand did not impact the very thin veneer of white settlement in just a handful of places. However, at the moment that an armed and restive Māori population began to potentially threaten European interests, the authorities acted, and legal limitations on the sale of firearms to the Māori began to creep into the territorial statute. The first of these was the "Arms, Gunpowder and other Warlike Stores Act of 1845," followed in 1846 by the "Arms Ordinance," and later still the "Gunpowder Ordinance Act 1847."

These limitations, the exhaustion of the warring groups, and a general spread of the rule of law put an end to much of the fighting, and while there was no truly official end for the Musket Wars, the fighting was largely over by 1842. During the thousands of individual skirmishes and battles, somewhere between 20,000-40,000 Māori lost their lives.[5] The end of the Musket Wars also marked the point that white interests and priorities began to predominate.

Missionaries and Whalers

"[T]he signal for the dawn of civilization, liberty, and religion in that dark and benighted land."
- Reverend Samuel Marsden, 1814

As was the case in almost every British overseas territory, the vanguard of settlement and pacification was the Christian missionary movement. The nationality and denomination of early hunters and traders invariably tended to influence the language and denomination of the first

---
[5] The Musket Wars were also known as the "Potato Wars." The name "Potato Wars" refers to the introduction of potatoes at about the same time as muskets which allowed for enough of a food surplus for iwi to concentrate on warfare with less effort needed to provide food.

missionaries, but it was always the missionaries who tested the waters and prepared the ground for future arrivals, founding the basic infrastructure of settlements and preparing the way for the establishment of formal dependencies.

They also, in many respects, provided a cultural bridge between the old and the new. The natives of any such territory, in this case the Māori, were introduced to the religion, language, and culture of the newcomers long before the pressures and realities of a colonial annexation were felt. The price of this was conversion, and the systematic destruction of traditional lifestyles, practices, and values. The spread of Christianity by this means depended often on the state of mind of those being converted. In Africa, for example, the absolute destruction by slavery and white rule of traditional societies created a vacuum, and Christianity filled that vacuum. Conversely, in places like India and New Zealand, indigenous belief structures remained strong, and Christianity did not make quite the same robust headway.

In the late 1700s, Christianity was superficially introduced to New Zealand by early traders and settlers, but this was simply by osmosis, not by conversion. It was not until 1814, when the first Protestant missionaries, members of the British Anglican Church Missionary Society, arrived on the shores of the two islands that formal Christianity appeared. The enterprise was delayed a little by an event known as the Boyd Massacre, which took place in 1809. The *Boyd* was a convict ship that sailed from Port Jackson in October 1809 to collect a cargo of timber from Whangaroa Harbor on the northern tip of North Island. For reasons that have never been clear, the crew of the ship, up to 70 men, were overrun, killed and eaten by local Māori, one of the largest massacres of Europeans in the early history of New Zealand, and one of the bloodiest episodes of cannibalism on record.

An 1889 painting of the *Boyd* blowing up

Catholicism arrived on the islands somewhat later. It was first introduced by Irish and French seamen and traders, and some early missionary work was attempted, but the first organized Catholic mission did not appear in New Zealand until formally introduced by the French in the 1830s.

Missionaries usually followed the first trading contacts, and in this case whaling represented the first and most obvious economic attraction of New Zealand's coastal waters. The harvesting of whales was an enormous industry at the time, competing only with the harvesting of ivory in Africa as a wildlife commodity that fed the Industrial Revolution. Whale blubber was used in illumination, various types of fuel, in oils for industry and armaments, and in numerous food products. Bones were used for fashion, instrumentation and construction. As early as 1791, the first whaler, the *William and Anne*, under Captain Ebner Bunker, appeared in New Zealand waters. The *William and Anne* set sail from England in March 1791 as part of the "Third Fleet," transporting goods and convicts to the penal colony of New South Wales on Australia.[6] The hunt for sperm whales in the South Pacific was a brief side venture, and there is no record that any whales were actually caught.

Nonetheless, by the turn of the century, whaling had become a thriving industry along the coast of New Zealand, with British, American, and French fleets regularly visiting the islands. This

---

[6] The First, Second and Third Fleets were waves of convict transportation dispatched from England to New South Wales between 1787 and 1792.

had the effect of establishing a small fraternity of Māori crewmen who joined the ships when they arrived onshore, and others who became permanently engaged as maritime merchant crew. By the mid-19th century, more than 100 shore bases had been established, although by then whale populations had begun to decline, and diminished returns saw many of these settlements abandoned soon afterwards.

In the meanwhile, the *Britannia*, another ship of the Third Fleet disembarked 188 convicts in Port Jackson and intended to divert to China en-route back to England in order to collect a cargo of tea. Although nominally interested in whale blubber, a more lucrative cargo in the form of fur seal pelts presented itself as the *Britannia* cruised the west coast of South Island. Men were dropped off, and in 10 months they were able to amass a haul of 4,500 skins. Fur seals were also to be found in significant numbers in the Bass Strait, along the Great Australian Bight and on the south shore of Tasmania. It was not really until these sources had begun to diminish that the industry picked up in New Zealand, but by 1830, seals had been hunted almost to extinction along the entire coast of New Zealand, and hunting was eventually banned in 1926.

Following these early whalers, the first Church Missionary Society station was established by Reverend Samuel Marsden in the Bay of Islands on the northern peninsular of North Island. This became the site of the first identifiable European town in New Zealand, then known by the Māori name as *Kororāreka*, but now known as Old Russell. The mission and the settlement were established at the confluence of old trade contacts between various commercial seamen and the local Māori. The Māori produced potatoes and pork, and in exchange for these, firearms and other sundry trade goods were bartered.

Marsden

The missionaries, however, encountered a violent and dissolute settlement, made worse by the effects of the gun trade in the hinterland and the general state of insecurity of the surrounding countryside. Missionary relations with the administration in Sydney were uncooperative, and certainly there was little early interest among the Māori in any moral currency the missionaries might have to trade - the Māori wanted the salvation of guns, not Christ.

Nonetheless, by 1840, mission stations had been established at Kaitaia, Thames, Whangaroa, Waikato, Mamamata, Rotorua, Tauranga, Manukau and Poverty Bay. Schools and hospitals were built, and the first efforts to educate the Māori youth began. By 1840, over 20 stations had been founded, most of which were on North Island, and all of which, to a greater or lesser extent, later evolved into towns and cities.

In many respects, the missionaries competed with the traders and hunters for the hearts and minds of the Māori population. As an alternative to guns and alcohol, the missionaries offered conversion, the development of a written form of their language, basic education, health and sanitation, and improved farming methods. As already noted, the missionaries offered a sympathetic cultural bridge and a soft landing as European influence penetrated ever deeper into the Māori cultural hinterland.

Indeed, from this initial missionary experience, a great many reflections and memoirs found their way into print, and from these sources, it is clear that the mission establishment was very hostile to the forces of trade and colonization. Trade and colonization brought out the worst in both sides. White traders and settlers tended to introduce disease, alcohol, and firearms, which attracted the most violent and corrupted elements of Māori society. Sexually transmitted diseases were rife in these communities, and offspring born as a result of contact between the two sides found themselves shunned by both cultures.

The irony perhaps is that the missionaries introduced their own corrosive ideologies and practices, and they were no less disdainful of ancient traditional practice than any other. They were jealous of the moral turf, and they did not encourage unaffiliated white settlement. Nonetheless, as the forces of trade and colonization grew more organized and ubiquitous, the missionaries bent to the inevitable, and in the end they were instrumental in persuading the Māori leadership to accept the terms of the iconic "Treaty of Waitangi."

The Founding of a Colony

"Governor, you should stay with us and be like a father. If you go away then the French or the rum sellers will take us Māori people over." - Chief Hōne Heke

The British colony of New South Wales was founded in 1788 upon the arrival of what is known as the First Fleet. This was the first formal expedition to establish a penal colony on the east coast of Australia, then known as New Holland. At the same time, the commission of the first Governor of New Zealand, Captain Arthur Phillip, included a broad remit on administrative responsibility for an area vaguely defined as encompassing "all the islands adjacent in the Pacific Ocean within the latitudes of 10°37'S and 43°39'S." This overlapped most of New Zealand, with the exception of the southern half of South Island.

Phillip

In 1825, Van Diemen's Land, the future Tasmania, was detached to form a separate colony under domestic administration, and as part of the reshuffle, the boundary of New South Wales was extended to include the islands adjacent in the Pacific Ocean, with a southern boundary of 39°12'S. This diminished the area of New Zealand under the control of New South Wales to only the northern half of North Island.

None of this was of much consequence on the ground since the extension of administrative control from Sydney was in any case academic. Interest at the time was focused on the mainland of *Terra Australis*, and developing the various settlements that sprung up on sundry parts of the Australian coast. There were, however, pockets of permanent white settlement taking place in a disordered and irregular manner, and there were, of course, the first shoots of missionary settlement. New Zealand became a popular destination for British fugitives from justice since no formal law existed on the islands, and so the first formal inclusion of New Zealand under a British administrative remit was legal.

Various legal statutes originating in the British Imperial Parliament brought the territory of New Zealand effectively under British law. The "Murders Abroad Act of 1817" was one of these, and although it was not specifically aimed at New Zealand, it allowed the authorities in New South Wales to legally pursue fugitives in New Zealand, and to ensure that no corner of the region could be claimed as a safe haven from British justice. Typically it fell on the judiciary of New South Wales to enforce any application of this Act in New Zealand.

The Murders Abroad Act was followed up in 1823 by a much more muscular and specific article of legislation, the "New South Wales Act of 1823," which placed under the jurisdiction of the Supreme Court of New South Wales all of the New Zealand territories.

The first official British presence in New Zealand was the appointment of a Resident named James Busby, a Scottish born immigrant to Australia who took up his appointment in the Bay of Islands settlement in March 1833. An official Resident was a diplomatic position with no specific powers other than to observe and report, but some authority did come with this appointment, even if it was a long way short of a consular appointment or a governorship. This appointment came about largely as a consequence of ongoing complaints by members of the Church Missionary Society of rampant lawlessness in the various settlements of North Island.

James Busby was an interesting character, and his influence on the early constitutional development of New Zealand was quite profound. He was born in Scotland, the son of the influencial engineer John Busby, and arrived in New South Wales with his family in 1824 at the age of 22. He was a viticulturalist by inclination and training, and his were the first vines planted in Australia. He was 30 when he arrived in New Zealand, and he was immediately captivated by what he saw. He built a home at Waitangi, and there he planted a vineyard from where the first wine in the colony was produced, reaching production even before the vines planted earlier in New South Wales.

Busby

Besides founding the wine industries of both colonies, Busby's official duties were to protect British commerce, to arbitrate in any disputes, and to act as mediator between unruly settlers and the sometimes no less unruly Māori. This was necessary because the Māori of New Zealand were by no means the fractured and inoffensive Aborigines of Australia, who withered away at almost their first contact with whites. Contacts between the whites and the Māori in New Zealand had the potential to be very violent indeed, and the standard of lawlessness in New Zealand made New South Wales, notwithstanding its predominantly convict population, seem like a playground by comparison.

In 1835, a rumor reached Busby that a French nobleman, the Baron Charles Philippe Hippolyte de Thierry, was intending to declare French sovereignty over the islands of New Zealand, which, under international convention, if not law, would certainly have carried some weight.[7] As a Resident, Busby represented the British Crown on the islands only, and as yet no formal act of annexation had been taken. Wasting no time, Busby, who had established a good network of diplomatic relations with the various Māori iwi, drafted a declaration of independence, which was signed at a meeting of 35 chiefs controlling most of North Island. What was created was ostensibly "The United Tribes of New Zealand."

This was an audacious move, and it might, under different circumstances, have worked. No French baron in the end had any real chance of securing control of the islands, but the possibility of an independent confederation of Māori tribes was intriguing, and bearing in mind the advanced state of development of the Māori, it was not utterly inconceivable. A similar attempt by the Australian Aborigines would have reaped such howls of derision that no one would have ever thought to try it. Māori emissaries and diplomats, on the other hand, had already visited New South Wales and England, and they were engaged on a diplomatic level with the ruling establishments of both. The Māori were engaged in international trade, some owned ships, some were educated, and in the absence of any other form of government on the island, the idea of a Māori government on some level was not treated as being utterly outlandish.

It is probably worth noting that the British Imperial Government, then at a fairly formative phase, would in quite a number of cases overlay British imperial superintendence over a native government as a means of administering a territory or dependency indirectly. The best example of this might be the "Dual Mandate" concept of Lord Frederick Lugard, in the British protectorate of Northern Nigeria. There, the various sultanates and emirates of the region remained intact, ruling in a manner disturbed only by very loosely applied British supervision. The advantage of this to the British was that their government came at a cheap price, and to the traditional leadership, access to modern systems of administration and government, compatible with any other, came without any radical modification to the traditional system.

---

[7] Baron de Thierry was in fact intending to establish a settlement, not a colony, which is somewhat different, but Busby made use of the rumor nonetheless.

Busby's declaration of independence entered a gray legal area, and in most instances, it was regarded as a curiosity without any particular force. It was rewarded with recognition from nowhere, and if it did have legal merit, that fell away with the later signing of the "Treaty of Waitangi." The signing of this treaty was one of the seminal milestones of New Zealand constitutional history, and it is a fascinating example of not only the inexorability, but also the adaptability of British imperial expansion.

From 1835-1840, the Colonial Office dithered over precisely what to do with New Zealand. In the spring of 1836, the Governor of New South Wales, Sir Richard Bourke, dispatched a naval expedition under the command of Captain William Hobson to visit New Zealand in order to investigate firsthand the situation in the territory. Hobson's recommendation was simply that British sovereignty be declared over limited areas of British and European settlement, with a view then to an incremental increase in claims over the entire territory. This report was forwarded to the Colonial Office for consideration, and in the spring of 1838, a House of Lords Select Committee met to consider the "State of the Islands of New Zealand." Submissions were made by various bodies, including private, public, commercial, and religious interests. This resulted in Letters Patent issued to expand the territorial scope of New South Wales to include both the North and South Islands of New Zealand in their entirety. The Governor of New South Wales, then Sir George Gipps, was formally given the additional responsibility of Governor of New Zealand.

Hobson

This, then, was the first clear statement of intent on the part of the British Imperial Government that it intended to make a formal claim over New Zealand. Prior to this, Hobson's suggestion of limited British sovereignty was weighed up, and although very nearly reaching a consensus, did not quite. The idea as it was discussed in Whitehall was simply for a "Māori State," perhaps even a republic, within which British settlers were guaranteed certain rights of land and representation. In the end, a full settler state was agreed to, and in practical terms, the declaration of independence was immediately rendered moot.

Hobson was then appointed British Consul to New Zealand, and to him fell the task of establishing the constitutional framework of a new colony, and also of negotiating the surrender of Māori sovereignty to the British Crown. Under instructions from the Home Secretary, the Marquis of Normanby, Hobson was to "seek a cession of sovereignty, to assume complete control over land matters, and to establish a form of civil government." No draft treaty was given to him to work with, however, so he was left largely to his own resources to create the necessary instruments.

The official British position, as these steps were being taken, was ostensibly to protect Māori interests. This idea lay very much at the fore of the imperial establishment at the time. The traditional view of the British Empire is that it was a rapacious, exploitative and violent institution that left the destroyed remains of native society in its wake. This was more the attitude of the settler communities themselves, and quite often the Imperial Government was at odds with overseas colonies over precisely this question. In 1837, for example, a British Parliamentary Select Committee sat to examine the state and condition of all aboriginal subjects of Her Majesty. The Committee met "to consider what measures ought to be adopted with regards to the native inhabitants of the countries where British settlements are made, and to the neighboring tribes, in order to secure to them the due observance of justice, and the protection of their rights; to promote the spread of civilization among them, and to lead them to the peaceful and voluntary reception of the Christian religion."

This was something of a clarion call to missionaries and administrators across the British Empire to pay greater heed to the effects that European settlements were having on the native races of the world. This concern was expressed largely for the natives of North America, the Hottentot of the Cape, and the Aborigines of Australia. The Māori were not held to be in quite the same class as these, and they were not regarded as imperiled in any way, but nonetheless, it was a sensitive issue, and the Imperial Government felt the need to tread warily.

On January 29, 1840 William Hobson arrived in the Bay of Islands, with a ship of the recently chartered New Zealand Company, the *Cuba*, arriving not far behind. This ship carried Company members commissioned to conduct a survey on the feasibility of organized settlement, and to break ground prior to the arrival of shiploads of assisted immigrants. Already anchored in the harbor was the *Aurora*, carrying the first of these Company settlers. The New Zealand Company was anxious to get all of this done and to take up land before British annexation and the complications that would follow.

The next day was a Thursday, and Hobson wasted no time in calling a general meeting at Christs Church at Kororāreka. By presenting the Letters Patent of 1839, he announced the establishment of British sovereignty, confirmed his own appointment and let it be known that a process of establishing the constitutional basis of the new colony would commence immediately.

The basis of any style of colony could only be consequent to some sort of agreement by treaty with the various Māori iwi. This was clearly understood by all parties, and it cannot therefore be said that the Māori were duped into anything or negotiated with in bad faith. In general, the Māori were respectful of the British at that time. Many Māori served as crewmembers on British ships and thus traveled, with quite a number visiting England. As a result, they had a much clearer sense of the world than many other native peoples at that time. The British were a great maritime and trading nation, and the benefits and ramifications of a grand alliance with them were reasonably understood.

The treaty that followed was carefully drafted and amended by Hobson himself, assisted by Busby as official Resident and Hobson's private secretary James Freeman. None of these men were lawyers, however, so the basic structure of the treaty was borrowed from the text of various preexisting British treaties. It was ready for translation in just four days. From there it was handed over to the missionary Henry Williams, who, along with his son, was fluent in *Te Reo*, the lingua franca of the Māori. It was they who constructed the Māori version of the document. This was done overnight, and on February 5, 1840 it was ready for circulation among the various Māori chiefs.

Williams

In a single sentence of 216 words, Hobson introduced himself as a constituted functionary of Her Majesty Victoria, with powers to establish government, and to control and manage European settlement, both current and pending, and empowered moreover to treat with the Māori. Thereafter, as contained in three articles, all sovereignty was to be ceded to the British Crown, the Māori were guaranteed continued, undisturbed access to their lands and resources, the Crown reserved first right of preemption for any land alienated, and the Māori were guaranteed of all the rights and privileges owed to any other British subjects.

The translation of this document was inevitably imperfect, and in the years since, it has been examined minutely for any evidence of deliberate duplicity, but the findings in general have tended to suggest not. The English and Māori versions of the treaty document are substantially the same, except for one or two subtle differences that might bear accusations of intentional ambiguity. In fact, the difficulty that Henry Williams encountered was in the absence of appropriate Māori language to cover some of the concepts imparted. For example, in Article One, the English version stated that the chiefs were obliged to cede all rights and powers of sovereignty to the Crown, while in the Maori version, the implication is quite different. Here it states that Māori chiefs relinquish all "government" to the Crown, which, of course, implies

Crown responsibility for administration and not full and sovereign overlordship. No direct translation for "sovereignty" exists in Māori, simply because the Māori functioned on the level of individual tribes without any paramount ruler. In a second point, the jumbled and rather chaotic interpretation seems not to have conveyed clearly the concept of "preemption," and the question of land and land purchase as a whole.[8]

Nonetheless, it was this document that was presented to an assembly of northern chiefs inside an expansive marquee erected on the grounds of Busby's home in Waitangi. The document was read aloud, first in English by Hobson, and then in *Te Reo* by Henry Williams. Thereafter, for some five hours, the contents of the draft treaty were debated by the Māori chiefs, and most accounts of the episode tend to portray it as a fractious and angry interlude, with subtle divisions that were not easy for the whites to interpret. There was, for example, division between converted Catholic and Anglican members of the Māori leadership, and this was in part because the small Catholic mission fraternity, mainly French, but also Irish, had been at work urging the chiefs not to trust the British authorities. There was a general resistance to the notion of a "Governor," and the loss of land, and in some instances it was demanded that land already purchased or occupied be returned. That said, the arguments seemed to be formulaic and rather spurious in character, for when the time came to ratify the treaty, 45 chiefs of North Island, representing the majority, presented themselves to sign. In fact, they arrived a day early, on February 6, which forced Hobson to improvise a ceremony.

In the end, it would seem that a rather sophisticated interpretation of the situation convinced the chiefs that the likely benefits of British sovereignty and protection would outweigh the disadvantages. It is also true that those gathering to debate the matter understood quite clearly the international dynamic now at play. If the British were denied constitutional sovereignty by treaty, then they would achieve it in some other way, probably by conquest, and the terms might then not be so generous. Moreover, there were always the French, occupying Polynesian islands where and when they could. Given a chance, they would certainly make a play for New Zealand, and in the grand scheme of things, the British were preferred.

Thus, on February 6, 1840, the "Treaty of Waitaki" was signed, and Busby's home thus acquired the name "Treaty House." Further signatures were later added, and on May 21, 1840, sovereignty was declared over North Island on the basis of the Waitaki Treaty, and over South Island by virtue of prior discovery by Captain James Cook in 1769.

For the time being, however, the colony of New Zealand remained subject to the administrative control of New South Wales, and Hobson was appointed Lieutenant Governor answerable to the Governor of New South Wales. The "Charter for Erecting the Colony of New Zealand" was issued by Letters Patent on November 16, 1840 which stated in its preamble that New Zealand

---

[8] "Preemption" is described by the Oxford Dictionary as the purchase of goods or shares by one person or party before the opportunity is offered to others.

would gain the status of the crown Colony separate from New South Wales on July 1, 1841.

Immigration and Settlement

"[F]raudulent debtors…have escaped from their creditors in Sydney or Hobart Town, and needy adventurers from the two colonies, almost unequally unprincipled." – John Dunmore Lang

For a long time, New Zealand was regarded purely as a commercial resource of New South Whales, and most of the early economic activity that increasingly introduced permanent settlement to the islands originated in New South Wales. It was merchants from Sydney, and later Hobart who pioneered the flax, timber, fur seal and whaling industries, and Sydney was the base from which the first Christian missions found their way to New Zealand.

The first recorded permanent settlement was in Dusky Sound, in 1792, located amongst the beautiful fjords of South Island. This was an insubstantial settlement that did not survive long. The 1825 settlement of Codfish Island, to the northwest of Stewart Island, in the extreme south of South Island, lasted a little longer, but it was soon shifted across the strait to Stewart Island, and then on to the mainland. These were all sealing and whaling depots, without any particular pretense at permanence. Those that began the exploit the timber reserves of the islands, concentrated mostly along the windward slopes of South Island, and in pockets of North Island, became the first of what might be regarded as permanent settlements. The timber of the region offered up a very necessary resource in the age of wooden ships, and once discovered, an organized timber industry, centered in Sydney, quickly kicked into gear. By 1816, the first cargoes of timber sawn and processed in New Zealand by permanently settled sawyers began to arrive in Sydney.

A census conducted in 1836 revealed that fully a third of all permanently settled European males in New Zealand were engaged in timber processing and export. Shore-based whaling operations were established soon afterwards, mainly along the east coast from Foveaux Strait, at the southern tip of South Island, to East Cape, the eastern-most point of North Island. By 1830, or thereabouts, some fifteen Sydney based firms and companies were managing twenty-two separate whaling settlements within this region. Some of these were quite substantial, for example in the Bay of Plenty, but others were sparsely populated and transitory.

The demographic was mixed, with many Māori engaged, and a steady interaction between settler men and Māori women occurred, with the inevitable result. Convicts, army and navy deserters and many others made up a population mainly of men, somewhat predisposed to violence and crime, and inclined towards dissolute habits. Fugitive convicts from the penal settlements of Australia were recorded in the Bay of Islands as early 1815, a fact observed by Charles Darwin when he visited the site in 1835. In 1837, the *Sydney Herald* estimated a population of between 200 and 300 escaped convicts in New Zealand, mainly in the Bay of Islands.

Among these were a group known as the *Pākehā Māori*, from the word Pākehā, the general Māori term for a white or European person. The Pākehā Māori were simply white men forced for one reason or another to take refuge in Māori communities, beyond the reach of British justice. One can assume, therefore, that most of these were escaped convicts and general fugitives although there certainly were those who entered that life as a matter of preference and were content within it. In rare instances, whites were held by the Māori as slaves although this certainly was rare. The number of Pākehā Māori in 1830 was about fifty, and a decade later about 150. Most were either English or Irish, and a majority appear to have rejoined white society more or less as British sovereignty was declared.

The missionaries, of course, represented another demographic, and as we have already heard, the first permanent missionaries arrived as part of the Church Missionary Society initiative, led by the Reverend Samuel Marsden in 1814. Many of the dispersed mission stations that were seeded from the initial settlement in the Bay of Islands became the basis of later towns and cities. On the eve of British sovereignty in 1840, Church and Wesleyan Missionary Society missionaries, and their families, numbered 206.

Then there were the free settlers, a sporadic addition to the commercial and missionary populations, and again mostly drifting across from New South Wales and other Australian settlements. The pace of free immigration began to quicken as the date of British annexation neared. This was partly because the establishment of a British colony required not only the recruitment of administrative personnel to take up various functions of government and the judiciary, but also because the development of a capital and the various construction and building projects associated with this further demanded the importation of skilled labor, many of whom brought their families. It is also true that land occupied prior to annexation was generally regarded as a *fait accompli*, so there were many attempting to gain land before a British administration could be introduced on the islands.

All of this also happened to coincide with the drought in New South Wales, the steady increase in the price of land and diminishing scope for settlement. The Swan River Settlement in Western Australia, a bold experiment in systematic settlement, had fared poorly, and a number of disappointed colonists from this region eventually made their way to New Zealand. New Zealand offered a new land with fresh opportunities, and as the century progressed, many people were alerted to this.

The first capital of New Zealand was Old Russell, now the small settlement of Okiato, some five miles south of present-day Ruddell in the Bay of Islands. In 1841, after the signing of the Treaty of Waitaki, the seat of government was shifted to the settlement of Auckland, named after the then Viceroy of India, the Earl of Auckland. The land was gifted to the government by the Ngāti Whātua, a local iwi as a gesture of goodwill.

Settlements were already beginning to form at Wellington and Nelson, in the Cook Strait, and recognizing in due course that the former offered a more central location for the administration of both islands, the territorial capital was moved to Wellington in 1865.

The attributes of New Zealand as a destination for British emigration were by the first decades of the 19th century well appreciated. The islands, in particular North Island, enjoyed a temperate climate suitable for European settlement, and fertile soils that were well drained and watered. Several attempts were made to organize systematic settlement, and although ultimately unsuccessful, they did succeed in introducing small numbers of fresh arrivals.

The first attempt was made in 1825, with the founding of the New Zealand Association, established in England to facilitate immigration to New Zealand, and to seek entry on a large scale into the flax, timber, whaling and fur industries. Somewhat as a by-product of this, organized immigration was also part of the New Zealand Association's plan. The New Zealand Association was superseded in 1825 by the New Zealand Company, which was not awarded its Royal Charter until 1841. At its founding, the Company unsuccessfully petitioned the British Imperial Government for a thirty-one-year period of exclusive trade, along with the right to settle the territory, and establish an army. Royal chartered companies were typically granted rights along these lines, examples of which, of course, are the Hudson Bay Company and the British East India Company. Trade in New Zealand was already dispersed quite widely by then, and a monopoly simply would not have been possible. The use of private armies, along the lines of the Indian Army, was not an attractive idea in New Zealand, because war would have been inevitable, and the British Imperial Government would have been required inevitably to intercede.

Nevertheless, the following year, the New Zealand Company dispatched two ships, the *Lambton* and the *Isabella*, under the command of Captain James Herd, to examine trade prospects and identify potential settlements. Sometime in September or October of 1826, the two ships dropped anchor in the Cook Straits, in present day Wellington Harbor which was very quickly established as a suitable site for permanent settlement. A million acres of land was supposedly purchased from the Māori although no documentation to this effect is in existence, and certainly nothing came of it.

The next venture of this kind, also underwritten by the New Zealand Company, was the voyage of the ship *Tory*, which anchored in Port Nicholson in August 1939, also with a view to identifying and purchasing likely sites for organized settlement. The first immigrant ship, the *Aurora*, of which we have already heard, arrived in Wellington Harbor in January 1840. Named after the Duke of Wellington, the proposed settlement was part of the New Zealand Companies model of organized colonization. This model, incidentally, was conceived and developed by Edward Gibbon Wakefield, a colorful character who was involved in quite a number of similar schemes in Australia and Canada before his engagement with the New Zealand Company.

Again, part of the haste in reforming the New Zealand Company, and then attempting to establish settlements in New Zealand had to do with pending British Imperial plans to establish a crown colony in New Zealand, after which the freebooting acquisition of land would be impossible. Wakefield, by then a forty-three-year-old adventurer with a highly checkered past, was invited to join the Company as a director. His philosophy was simply, *"Possess yourself of the Soil and you are Secure."*[9]

The Wakefield Plan simply envisaged packages of land comprising a "town acre," accompanied by 100 country acres, and 1,100 such one-acre town sections were planned for Port Nicholson. This, then, became the basis for the settlement and establishment of Wellington, followed in 1840 by Wanganui, in 1841 by New Plymouth and Nelson in 1842. Some efforts were also made to survey possible sites on South Island. The economic basis of all of this was the idea that large tracts of land would be acquired by purchase from the Māori which would then be parceled up for sale to prospective immigrants.

The Company quickly ran into financial difficulties. For the plan to succeed, higher land prices would need to attract reasonably wealthy colonists whose land purchases would then fund the free immigration of those needed to work the land and build the settlements. In the end there always seemed to be more impoverished immigrants subscribing for assisted passage than those willing to pay for it. In 1844, the Company ceased active trading, and surrendered its charter in 1850. The Company's debts were initially assumed by the British Government, but these were passed on to the New Zealand government in 1854.

Nonetheless, a momentum had begun, and over the next few years, over 8,600 colonists arrived in New Zealand in some 57 ships. By 1859, non-Māori represented the majority population of New Zealand, with over 100,000 English, Scottish and Welsh immigrants permanently settled in New Zealand.

The New Zealand Wars

"They were so generous as to tell us they would come and attack us in the morning." – Captain James Cook

The years immediately following the signing of the Treaty of Waitaki were therefore characterized by a flood of European immigration and settlement, far more than those signatories to the Treaty, and their descendants, could ever have imagined. In 1845, the tensions and anxieties erupted into a series of conflicts known as the "Māori Wars," and more recently, the "New Zealand Wars."

The question at the root of this period of New Zealand history is whether a majority of those Māori leaders who signed the Treaty of Waitaki really understood what terms they were agreeing

---

[9] Edward Gibbon Wakefield was perhaps most widely known for an episode known as the "Shrigley Abduction," during which he abducted a fifteen-year-old heiress and forced her to marry him, for which he and his brother received a three-year prison sentence.

to. Even if they did, the terms included in the treaty were vague at best, and certainly no limits were imposed on the alienation of land, and nor the numbers of immigrants expected in the colony.

At its conception, the idea of limiting the sale of Māori land to the government, thereby banning any sale between two private parties, was primarily to protect the Māori from exploitation from the many agencies, the New Zealand Company among them, with an interest in acquiring large tracts. In general, the Māori sought trade with the Europeans, and land was a tradable commodity. The Māori as a race did not quite hold the land in the manner that the Australian aboriginal did, as a commonly held natural resource, as free to all as the air or the water, and so dealing with them over the matter of land acquisition was somewhat more give and take.

Inevitably, as the pace of immigration quickened, so the government began to come under increasing pressure to make land available for agriculture and settlement. In the 1850s, an organization known as the "Māori King Movement" or *Kīngitanga,* came into being in the central region of North Island, to resist the alienation of Māori land. What set the match to the tinder was the controversial 1859 purchase by Governor Colonel Sir Thomas Gore-Browne of a disputed block of land in the Waitara district in the southwest of North Island. The Kīngitanga resisted, and loudly protested, which Governor Gore-Browne, an imperious and belligerent character, interpreted as a direct challenge to his authority. Imperial troops were brought in from the various Australian colonies, and assisted by a force of some 4,000 colonial militias and *kupapa*, which were pro-government Māori militias, the government set about provoking a war.

The New Zealand Wars occurred over a wide span of time, with the first disturbances commencing almost at the moment that the ink on the Treaty of Waitaki was dry. The first major clash, for example, took place on 17 June 1843 in the Wairau Valley of the South Island, more or less on the opposite side of the Cook Strait from the new settlements of Wellington and Nelson. The antagonist in this instance was unsurprisingly the New Zealand Company. An attempt to clear Māori from the *Ngāti Toa* tribe off land acquired by fraudulent purchase prompted a clash that resulted in the killing of twenty-two settlers and four Māori. Several more Europeans were killed after being captured. An official investigation later concluded that the settlers had been at fault, and this probably had much to do with the fact that the office of the Governor was in general hostile to the activities of the New Zealand Company. Although obviously the Company was at fault, it was unusual for blame to be so unequivocally laid at the feet of whites. Nonetheless, Governor Robert Fitzroy contemplated for a while an armed expedition to the Wairau Valley, but in the end decided against it.

This affair, known as the Wairau Affray, of the Wairau Confrontation, was the first and only armed conflict between white and Māori to take place on South Island, and some historical accounts do not place it in the general frame of the New Zealand Wars.

The more sustained conflict was triggered on North Island in March 1845, under the governorship of George Grey, a career diplomat and colonial civil servant who held known sympathies for the native subjects of the Empire. He entered almost immediately into a difficult situation as tribal leaders began mounting a strong challenge against the authority of his office. The flagstaff on a hill above Kororāreka was cut down, and a military facility burned to the ground. The leader of these disturbances was Hōne Heke, chief of the Ngāpuhi iwi, and the essential grievance was again land acquisitions, this time by the Church Missionary Society. There was by then also a widely expressed and general contempt for the terms of the Treaty of Waitaki.

The conflagration was not universally supported, and only a minority of the Ngāpuhi were in fact involved. The defeat of the small British garrison, with a minor force of local levies, at the "Battle of Ohaeawai" tended to lend the business more gravity than was perhaps justified. Nonetheless, Governor Grey, better armed and better informed than his predecessor, pursued the rebels until they were forced to sue for peace. Pragmatic terms of peace were established, and none of the leaders suffered any particular punitive measure.

Almost at the moment that hostilities died down in what later came to be known as the "Flagstaff War," renewed tension broke out in the south of North Island, as something of a sequel to the Wairau Affray, and once again, dubious land purchases and enforced removal lay at the root. Settlers were anxious to gain physical occupation of land in the valley of the Hutt River before any disputes were settled. The Hutt River drains into Wellington Harbor, and the expansion was, of course, associated with the establishment of the Wellington settlement. The same protagonists fought several engagements, with British and settler forces supported by local levies, or *kūpapa*.[10] This was a dispersed, but violent and bloody campaign, with the Māori attacking and destroying homesteads and very much taking the fight to the British. The fighting was ended by a peace settlement in 1848.

And so it continued. There were at least nine distinct wars fought between 1845 and 1872 when the New Zealand Wars were said to be officially over. The common theme of all of the individual incidences was land, land ownership, land seizure and land alienation. The initial disturbances tended to be localized, but after 1860, the scope and intensity of the conflict intensified to the extent that the government began to believe that an orchestrated and general Māori uprising was beginning to take shape. To deal with it, an appeal was made for Imperial troops, and a major and orchestrated British military campaign was mounted to neutralize the Kīngitanga, or "Māori King Movement." A secondary, and perhaps even a primary objective of this campaign, was to acquire through conquest yet more land for an ever-growing settler population.

---

[10] There were many reasons why Māori kūpapa sided with the British. In some cases it was because of genuine support for the British; in others for the sake of local and regional advantage. The use of native levies and constabularies was a mark of European colonial expansion, and a great many colonial wars were little more than civil wars.

At the height of hostilities, some 18,000 British troops were involved in operations, supported by detachments of kūpapa, and numerous ad hoc settler militias dealing with more localized equalization. The British fielded cavalry and artillery, and were opposed by a combined force of no more than 4,000 Māori warriors. The objective was obviously to once and for all crush Māori resistance, and to gain free and uninhibited access to the land.

The Māori were able to mount an effective resistance only by making use of their superior local knowledge and fluency with local conditions. The war devolved eventually into guerrilla-style conflicts that favored neither side, but which, in the end tilted in the direction of the British, simply because of superior numbers, capability and logistics. Over the course of the Taranaki and Waikato campaigns, for example, about 1,800 Māori were killed against 800 British, and total Māori losses during the combined conflict certainly exceeded 2,000, and in fact, the official Māori death toll, including civilians, was 2,154, which, out of a peak deployment of 5,000, amounted to a very heavy combined loss.

In 1863, the New Zealand Settlement Act was passed, ostensibly to formalize the chaotic events of the previous two decades, but in practical terms it simply legalized the confiscation of land as a de facto punishment for the rebellion. Land confiscation was somewhat arbitrary, directed at loyal and hostile   Māori groups, and was really nothing more than a mass appropriation. More than 6,200 square miles of Māori land was seized in the aftermath of the Act. This had the additional effect of removing the main source of support and refuge for Māori rebels and holdouts.

All of this provided a basis for the end of the New Zealand Wars, and the orchestrated settlement of incoming Europeans across most of the islands. It would not be the end of the matter, however, and the legacy of land seizure and acquisition during this period remains a live issue today, and a lengthy program of reevaluation and adjustments to land ownership are ongoing today.

Colonial Government

"It was Junior England all the way to Christchurch." – Mark Twain

Upon the formal annexation of New Zealand by the British Imperial Government, the territory was established as an administrative extension of the colony of New South Wales, but by 1941, the territory existed as a colony in its own right. Its political practices and traditions, of course, were directly inherited from the British. The Crown was represented by a governor, who was advised by an appointed legislative council, and not, initially at least, a representative council. This did not take place until 1852, with the passing of the New Zealand Constitution Act, which provided for the establishment of an elected house of representatives and a legislative council. The first meeting of the General Assembly, a combined sitting of the House and Council, took place in 1854.

By this, New Zealand was self-governing in almost every respect, with the exception of foreign affairs and defense, but also, crucially, in anything related to native affairs and native policy. This, by then, had become a reasonably common policy in British imperial administration, and much of the reason for it had to do with the fact that the Imperial Government simply did not place enough trust in its settler communities overseas to deal equally and fairly with matters of land and resources in relation to natives, tribes and peoples. In New Zealand, this would remain the case until the late 1860s, as the New Zealand Wars were tailing off, at which point the comprehensive and legal settlement of many of the associated issues began.

The provincial structure of the colony initially included three provinces, and these were New Ulster (North Island, north of the Patea River), New Munster (North Island, south of Patea River, plus South Island) and New Leinster (Stewart Island). These were amended under the New Zealand Constitution Act 1852, and six new provinces were established, namely Auckland, New Plymouth, Wellington, Nelson, Canterbury and Otago. Each was empowered with its own legislature that elected its own speaker and superintendent. The franchise was extended to anyone of twenty-one years or older, owning freehold property worth £50 or more.

Between November 1858 and December 1873, four additional provinces were introduced, and these were Hawkes Bay, Marlborough, Westland and Southland. Soon after the establishment of these new subdivisions, the whole concept of provinces was debated and eventually removed. Under the premiership of Harry Atkinson, tenth premier of New Zealand, the Abolition of Provinces Act of 1876 was passed which replaced provinces with regions.

This, then, was the constitutional character of New Zealand as the colony approached the dawn of the 20th century. The territory had been comprehensively pacified, the Māori put in their place, but the land itself remained largely unexplored and very sparsely understood. Naturalists and explorers found themselves confronted by a wild and enigmatic land, filled with exotic flora and fauna found nowhere else, and while the bloody business of claiming the land was underway, there were many other Europeans wandering the land, mapping it, exploring it and trying to understand its intricacies. In the next in this series we will look at natural New Zealand, and how it was brought into the European frame of knowledge and understanding.

Appendix: The Treaty of Waitangi

HER MAJESTY VICTORIA Queen of the United Kingdom of Great Britain and Ireland regarding with Her Royal Favor the Native Chiefs and Tribes of New Zealand and anxious to protect their just Rights and Property and to secure to them the enjoyment of Peace and Good Order has deemed it necessary in consequence of the great number of Her Majesty's Subjects who have already settled in New Zealand and the rapid extension of Emigration both from Europe and Australia which is still in progress to constitute and appoint a functionary properly authorized to treat with the Aborigines of New Zealand for the recognition of Her Majesty's Sovereign authority over the whole or any part of those islands – Her Majesty therefore being desirous to establish a settled form of Civil Government with a view to avert the evil consequences which must result from the absence of the necessary Laws and Institutions alike to the native population and to Her subjects has been graciously pleased to empower and to authorize me William Hobson a Captain in Her Majesty's Royal Navy Consul and Lieutenant-Governor of such parts of New Zealand as may be or hereafter shall be ceded to her Majesty to invite the confederated and independent Chiefs of New Zealand to concur in the following Articles and Conditions.

Article the first [Article 1] The Chiefs of the Confederation of the United Tribes of New Zealand and the separate and independent Chiefs who have not become members of the Confederation cede to Her Majesty the Queen of England absolutely and without reservation all the rights and powers of Sovereignty which the said Confederation or Individual Chiefs respectively exercise or possess, or may be supposed to exercise or to possess over their respective Territories as the sole sovereigns thereof.

Article the second [Article 2] Her Majesty the Queen of England confirms and guarantees to the Chiefs and Tribes of New Zealand and to the respective families and individuals thereof the full exclusive and undisturbed possession of their Lands and Estates Forests Fisheries and other properties which they may collectively or individually possess so long as it is their wish and desire to retain the same in their possession; but the Chiefs of the United Tribes and the individual Chiefs yield to Her Majesty the exclusive right of Preemption over such lands as the proprietors thereof may be disposed to alienate at such prices as may be agreed upon between the respective Proprietors and persons appointed by Her Majesty to treat with them in that behalf.

Article the third [Article 3] In consideration thereof Her Majesty the Queen of England extends to the Natives of New Zealand Her royal protection and imparts to them all the Rights and Privileges of British Subjects.

(signed) William Hobson, Lieutenant-Governor.

Now therefore We the Chiefs of the Confederation of the United Tribes of New Zealand being assembled in Congress at Victoria in Waitangi and We the Separate and Independent Chiefs of New Zealand claiming authority over the Tribes and Territories which are specified after our respective names, having been made fully to understand the Provisions of the foregoing Treaty, accept and enter into the same in the full spirit and meaning thereof in witness of which we have attached our signatures or marks at the places and the dates respectively specified. Done at Waitangi this Sixth day of February in the year of Our Lord one thousand eight hundred and forty.

Online Resources

Other British history titles by Charles River Editors

Other titles about New Zealand on Amazon

Bibliography

James Belich, Making Peoples: A History of the New Zealanders from the Polynesian settlement to the end of the nineteenth century (1996)

James Belich, Paradise Reforged: A History of the New Zealanders from 1880 to the Year 2000 (2001).

Giselle Byrnes, ed. (2009). The New Oxford History of New Zealand. Oxford University Press.

Michael King (2003) The Penguin History of New Zealand.

Leveridge, Steven. "Another Great War? New Zealand interpretations of the First World War towards and into the Second World War" First World War Studies (2016) 7#3:303-25.

Parsons, Gwen. "The New Zealand Home Front during World War One and World War Two." History Compass 11.6 (2013): 419-428.

Smith, Philippa Mein. A Concise History of New Zealand (Cambridge Concise Histories) (2nd ed. 2012)

Keith Sinclair, ed., (1996) The Oxford Illustrated History of New Zealand.

Keith Sinclair, A History of New Zealand.

Ranginui Walker (2004), Ka Whawhai Tonu Matou: Struggle Without End.

Free Books by Charles River Editors

We have brand new titles available for free most days of the week. To see which of our titles are currently free, click on this link.

Discounted Books by Charles River Editors

We have titles at a discount price of just 99 cents everyday. To see which of our titles are currently 99 cents, click on this link.

Made in United States
North Haven, CT
07 December 2022